Summer of the Werewolf

Kevin Philbin

Stanley Thornes (Publishers) Ltd

Originally published in 1983 by Hutchinson Education
Reprinted 1984, 1988

Reprinted in 1990 by
Stanley Thornes (Publishers) Ltd
Old Station Drive
Leckhampton
CHELTENHAM GL53 0DN

British Library Cataloguing in Publication Data
Philbin, Kevin
Summer of the Werewolf
1. Readers
I. Title
428.6'2 PE1121

ISBN 0 7487 0250 4

Cover photographs by Hamill Photo Services
and the Science Photo Library

Printed and bound in Great Britain at Martin's of Berwick

1

The whole thing was a mess. There was no other word for it. The baby was due at any moment but the new house wasn't going to be ready for at least another month. We were living in digs at the time and the new tenant should have moved in weeks before.

The landlady came round every day to see when we were going. Honestly, if it had been Christmas you could easily have believed it to be the Jesus and Mary story all over again. You know, no room at the inn and all that sort of stuff.

It was actually June. A warm, damp, close sort of June. For most of the time Mum just sat in the big chair in the kitchen with tiny beads of sweat standing out on her fat, pink face. She looked like someone who'd just been for a bath and forgotten to dry themselves properly.

On the day we broke up for the half-term holiday Mum fainted. The doctor had just left when I got home and Dad was waiting for me in the kitchen. He looked worried.

'Sandra,' he said after I'd finished my tea, 'If I asked you to do me a big favour do you think you'd do it?' He took hold of my hands and squeezed them. 'Just for your old Dad?'

'You know I would,' I told him. 'I want you and Jimmy to go away for a while. Just until the baby arrives and the new house is sorted out.'

Jimmy's my step-brother. He's thirteen – two years younger than me. He's my step-brother because Vi isn't my real mum. My mum's dead. He was starting his half-term holiday too.

'Where will we go?' I asked Dad. 'Down to Vi's Auntie Beth in Cornwall,' he said. 'It won't be for long. I promise.'

I didn't say anything for a while. I was trying to remember what Auntie Beth was like. I'd only met her once. Years ago at the wedding. All I could remember was that she was very old and that she walked with a stick. 'Well?' Dad said. I nodded. Dad grabbed hold of me and gave me a hug. 'Good girl,' he whispered. 'I knew I could rely on you.'

I felt so miserable I could have gone to bed and cried for a week.

2

It took ages getting there. First, we had to catch one train to London and then another to Penzance. From there we had to catch two buses and after all that we had to walk for about half a mile. Of course, Jimmy was no company at all. I mean, he's a nice enough kid but he just doesn't say much. He's always got a book stuck in front of him. I think he's quite a brainy kid really. He's into collecting stamps and all that sort of thing. Anything like that drives me round the bend.

It was dark by the time we got there. There was a nice silvery moon in the sky and the whole place looked really pretty and peaceful.

Auntie Beth had waited up for us. She stoked up the fire and brewed some tea the minute we arrived. So she couldn't be all bad. When we got in she put down her stick and gave each of us a kiss. She had really rough skin, like a man, and she smelled all sort of milky – rather like a baby.

She asked us about Mum and Dad, then told us to have a wash and go to bed. My room was freezing. I looked around for a fire – but there just wasn't one there. The bed was as hard as a rock and the room had a sort of musty, damp smell. I climbed into bed, put my head under the covers and tried to get to sleep. . . .

'Come along, Sandra dear. Breakfast is on the

table.' I lifted my head from the bed and looked up. Auntie Beth was standing at the door. She was wearing a tatty old dressing gown and her grey hair was all lank and messy, like an upturned mop. 'We don't want the tea to get cold. Do we?' she asked briskly. 'No,' I said trying to force a smile. I picked up my watch and looked at the time. It was 7.15. 'Some holiday,' I thought to myself.

Living at Auntie Beth's wasn't too bad really. Once you got used to the fact that it was nearly always cold, there was hardly ever any hot water and you had to be Tarzan just to pull the loo chain, you might even get to like it. Mind you I never did. All Auntie Beth seemed to do was get up at the crack of dawn and then sit in the kitchen all day scoffing tea and sandwiches made from stale bread.

We spent the first few days just getting to know the place. In the mornings we went shopping with Auntie Beth and in the afternoons we took a few sandwiches with us and went for long walks in the countryside. It really was a lovely place. A bit dead, but ever so pretty. Just like a postcard.

Auntie Beth went to get her pension on the Wednesday morning. We had to hang around outside for ages. I looked in a couple of times but there was no queue in the shop. There was just Auntie Beth and the woman behind the counter having a natter. When she came out she looked all excited. Her eyes were brighter and she looked more awake than she had done since we'd arrived. 'There's been some trouble!' she said the minute she got out of the shop door. 'Up on the hills over there.' She pointed to the low, green hills just behind the village.

'What kind of trouble?' I said, trying to sound interested.

'Sheep worrying. One of the local farmers found two of his sheep dead this morning. Their throats had been ripped open from ear to ear!' She drew her finger slowly across her throat. 'And not only that. The guts had been torn clean out of their bellies. They reckon it was a proper blood bath!' Just for a moment she looked like the Devil himself, I'm not kidding. She had a real wicked glint in her eyes.

'But that's terrible!' I said. 'They reckon it was a dog,' she went on, ignoring me. 'But it must be a real savage brute to do that. A real savage brute! Now,' she said, handing me one of the shopping bags, 'I want to get some bread from the baker and Mrs Adams said that she'd save me some of that cheap butter. Come on!' She toddled off down the street with Jimmy and me following her, just like a pair of sheep.

3

The next few days were hell. Auntie Beth had those dead sheep on her mind. It was horrible to think of how they died and it made her very nervous. She wanted to know where we were every minute of the day. She wouldn't let Jimmy go into the village without me and I knew that she worried when I went off by myself. I started to feel hemmed in. Trapped. It was a horrible feeling.

When we went shopping on the Friday I 'phoned home. Dad said that Mum was fine and he didn't think it would be long before the baby arrived. Sure enough, I 'phoned again on the Saturday afternoon and was told by the landlady that Mum had been taken into hospital. I couldn't 'phone the next day because it was Sunday and the Post Office was shut. You can imagine how the day dragged on. I hate Sundays even at the best of times – but this one seemed to last for about a week.

In the evening, just for something to do, I decided to finish unpacking. I'm so lazy I'd left everything in my case till then and just dragged it out when I needed it. So, I emptied the wardrobe completely, had a good nose at the old stuff I found at the back and then started to hang up my clothes. The time flew past. In fact, I was just finishing when I heard the church clock strike midnight.

That was when I saw the dagger.

It was a funny looking thing. About twenty centimetres long with rust spots all over the blade. But what was strange about it was the handle. It was shaped like a cross. The kind you see in churches. There was even a figure of Jesus on the cross. It was an odd thing to have on the handle of a dagger. It looked all wrong. A bit creepy really. The dagger was right at the top of the wardrobe. Stuck away at the back. Getting it wasn't going to be easy. I couldn't reach it from the bed so I pulled out the drawer at the bottom of the wardrobe and climbed on that.

I'd just grabbed the dagger when the wardrobe suddenly lurched forward and crashed to the floor. The noise it made seemed to shake the whole house. For a minute I just stood there terrified, waiting for Auntie Beth to come rushing into my room. I couldn't hear any movement in the rest of the house so I opened my bedroom door and went out into the hall.

Jimmy's bedroom was next to mine. Very quietly, I opened his door and looked in. The light wasn't on in his room but I could see quite clearly because the curtains were open and the room was flooded with moonlight. As I stood at the door the lace curtains moved softly in the night air. The bedroom window was wide open. I looked over at the bed. The covers had been pulled back. The bed was empty. I wasn't sure what to do for a moment. I went over to the window and looked out but I couldn't really see anything clearly in the darkness – just shadows.

I thought for a minute and then went to Auntie Beth's room. I knocked, but she didn't answer. I called her a couple of times but there was still nothing. So, I went in. At first I couldn't see anything – but I could hear her. She was snoring like a pig. The room was very dark and cold and smelled a bit of Auntie Beth. I turned on the light and went over to the bed. She was lying very still with her face turned upwards. I put my hand on her shoulder and shook her gently, but she still didn't wake up.

As I stood over her I noticed a large brown pill bottle on the bedside table. I picked it up and looked inside. It was full of tiny yellow tablets. There was a label on the front of the bottle. It was printed in red and it said:

SLEEPING PILLS
TAKE ONE TABLET PER NIGHT
ONLY

The word 'only' was underlined. I put the bottle back on the table, turned out the light and went back to my bedroom.

I tried to push the wardrobe back on to its feet but it was too heavy for me. When I gave up trying, I noticed that there was a small wooden box jammed in at the top corner, near to where the dagger had been. I picked it up and blew the muck off it. The dust on the top was like a carpet. The pattern on the lid of the box had faded but I could still make out bits of blue and red here and there. It looked a bit like an old jewellery box, but I couldn't be sure. When I opened it I saw that there was a piece of paper folded so that it would fit inside the box. There was also an old brown photograph of a small boy and a lock of curly black hair tied up with a bit of string.

I picked up the photo and stared at it. It had faded a lot but I could still make out the thin, sickly-looking face and the dark, curly hair. But what struck me most were the eyes. The boy in the photo had exactly the same eyes as Jimmy. Dark and frightened-looking. A bit like an animal when it gets trapped. In fact the more I looked at the photo the more I saw Jimmy in it. The boy in the photo was just like him.

The piece of paper began to tear along the folds as I opened it. It was dry and very brittle. When I finally got it open I saw that it was a note written in large, old-fashioned handwriting. Across the top was the date 23 June 1916. This is what it said:

They brought him home in the early hours of the morning. Father said that I was not to see him but I went to him while they were out digging the grave.

His poor face was twisted like a wild animal and the cruel knife was still deep in his chest. I lay my head over his broken body and wept so that my warm tears might wake him.

But he did not stir.

When I heard them coming to fetch him I pulled the dagger from his heart and cut off one of his darling curls so that I might have something to remember him by. My own dear son, my Matthew. May God have mercy on his soul.

In the stillness of the night I suddenly felt cold and empty and tired. I looked down at the dagger on the floor but I couldn't bring myself to touch it. I was sure that this was the dagger that had killed Matthew, the boy in the photograph. What I didn't understand was how the boy had died. Why was his face twisted like a wild animal's? And why had he been killed with such a strange dagger?

In the back of my mind the answers to these questions started to form – but they were too terrible to put into words. I only knew that when I looked at the photo again and saw how alike Matthew and Jimmy were I suddenly felt very, very scared.

I lay back on the bed and tried to listen for Jimmy coming back – but I must have fallen asleep. When I woke again it was morning.

4

I made sure I was out of my bedroom before Auntie Beth came in and saw the wardrobe. As I was going downstairs I saw Jimmy come out of his room. 'Where the hell were you last night?' I shouted up to him. Jimmy just stopped at his door and looked down at me. 'In bed of course,' he said quietly. 'No you weren't. You went to bed but you didn't stay there. Did you? You got up in the middle of the night and started playing silly beggars! Climbing out of your bedroom window!'

'What's all this shouting about?' I looked down and saw Auntie Beth coming out of the kitchen. 'I hope you two aren't going to start fighting now that you're here. I don't think my nerves could take that.' Maybe I should have told her about Jimmy going out in the night. I don't know why I didn't, but I didn't. 'It's nothing,' I muttered. 'It's just Jimmy being stupid again!' 'Now, now Sandra,' Auntie Beth said. 'Let's all have our breakfast and try to forget it. Whatever it is.' 'I want to have a word with you later,' I said to Jimmy just before we went into the kitchen.

Things were getting on top of me a bit that morning. I wanted to find out just what Jimmy had been up to in the night and I had to make sure I got the wardrobe back in place before Auntie Beth saw it. But most of all I wanted to 'phone home and find out about the baby.

In the end the baby won. As soon as I had finished breakfast I dashed out of the house and down into the village to the Post Office. I asked Jimmy if he wanted to come but he said he didn't.

A blue police van pulled up outside the Post Office just as I got there. Two policemen with dogs climbed out of the back of the van and then it sped off out of the village.

'It's not safe for a young girl like you to come all the way into the village alone,' the woman in the Post Office said to me as I went in. 'It's not safe for any of us come to that. Nobody has seen that thing that's killing all the sheep yet. For all you know it might be something that's escaped from a zoo. A lion or maybe a bear even. If it can kill a sheep, it might kill a person.'

'All I want to do is use the 'phone,' I said trying to shut her up.

'Do you want me to ask one of those policemen to walk back with you?' she pointed to the two men outside. 'No thanks,' I said quickly. 'One of them looks quite young,' she said with a smirk on her face. 'Don't you fancy him then?' I didn't even bother to answer her. I went over to the 'phone and picked it up.

While I was waiting for the 'phone to ring, a man came into the shop. He told the woman that two more sheep had been killed in the night. That was all I heard. The ringing stopped and Mum answered at the other end of the line. She was back at home.

Her trip to the hospital had been a false alarm. The baby might not be born for another week or so.

I didn't want to worry her so I didn't say anything about Jimmy going out in the night. I told her that we were both well and looking forward to coming back home. Then I said goodbye. 'You just be careful on your way back!' the shopkeeper called after me as I went out.

When I got home I didn't go straight into the house. It was a warm, sunny morning so I sat outside for a while. There was a big garden at the back of the house that led down to a stream. I sat down by the water's edge and thought about the baby. I was sorry that it hadn't been born. Partly because I was dying to find out if it was a boy or a girl and partly because it meant we would have to stay longer at Auntie Beth's. I was beginning to dislike this sleepy little village. It was starting to get me down.

As I sat there on the damp grass a small grey stone in the far corner caught my eye. It was sticking straight up out of the ground, just like a gravestone. I got up and went over to it. It was a gravestone. It looked ever so strange, standing there all alone. Not creepy, just sort of sad and lonely. As if everyone had forgotten about it. I knelt down and read the writing on the stone. It said:

MATTHEW CARTER
born 1903 died 1916
RIP

And that was it. The grass around the stone was smooth and flat, just like the rest of the garden. This was where they had buried him that night. This was the grave they had dug while his mother had cried over his body. I'm not the religious type but I just felt that I couldn't go away without doing something. So, I said a short prayer and then went into the house.

Auntie Beth was waiting for me. 'Have you got anything to say to me?' she asked as I walked in. For a moment I had no idea of what she was talking about. 'Do you go around smashing furniture in your own home?' she went on. 'Is that how you behave?'

'Oh the wardrobe,' I said. 'That's right. My good wardrobe. Now young lady,' she said waving her finger at me. 'So long as you stay in my house you'll show some respect for my things. If you break or damage anything else you tell me right away. Is that clear?' 'I was going to explain,' I told her. 'It's just that I didn't know what to say.'

'Sorry might have been a good place to start. Don't you think? Well?' She was waiting for me to say something. 'I'm sorry,' I said. 'I'll be more careful next time.' While she went off muttering to herself I went to look for Jimmy to get him to help me put the wardrobe back.

He was at the back door. There was a tiny black kitten with him and he was giving it some milk on one of Auntie Beth's plates. 'It might be a stray,' he said looking up at me. 'It was here yesterday. I gave it some milk then too.' 'Well, I hope it was on the same plate,' I said. 'I don't fancy eating my dinner off a plate that a cat has been licking.'

'It's all black,' he said quietly. 'Every bit of it. Just like a witch's cat. I'm going to call it Satan.' He couldn't have picked a dafter name. It looked more like a teddy bear than a devil. 'Come on!' I told him. 'I need you to help me shift my wardrobe.'

When we'd finally got the wardrobe back on its feet I asked him about the night before. He said that he couldn't remember anything – except going to bed and getting up in the morning. When I told him that his bed had been empty he just stood there looking stupid. I didn't know what to think. I wasn't sure if he was lying or telling the truth.

5

That afternoon we all went into the village shopping. On the way there I asked Auntie Beth about that grave in the garden. She seemed quite happy to talk about it so I let her rattle on. 'Matthew was my older brother,' she told me. 'I never knew him. I was just a baby when he died. There was a reason why he was buried out the back and not in the churchyard. But I can't think of it now. The war was on then you see. Nothing was normal at that time. Daddy died the same year in France. Fighting for his country. It must have been a terrible year for the family.'

'What did Matthew die of?' I asked. 'Fits.' By that time we had got to the village. We stopped talking about Matthew and started to sort out the shopping. There was quite a lot to do. We went to the supermarket, the butcher and the baker. When we got to the chemist Auntie Beth told us to wait outside for her. So I stood on the pavement and looked round at the village. There weren't many people about. Jimmy sat in the gutter, yawning.

After a short time an old woman came along. She was dressed in a ragged black coat and a red headscarf that looked as if it had been used for polishing shoes. She stopped when she got to me and reached out her filthy hand. 'Have you got 10p to buy an old woman a cup of tea?' she said. 'I haven't had a drop all day.' She smelt of stale beer. I reached down into my pocket and felt for a coin. All I had was a 50p. While I was feeling for something less, the old woman turned and saw Jimmy. For a long time she just stood there, staring at him. Then she said, 'I know you boy! I know you!' That was all.

Jimmy didn't say anything. I think the old woman had frightened him.

'I'm sorry I haven't got any money,' I said to her. She didn't turn round at first. She kept on looking at Jimmy. When at last she did look at me she said, 'When you come to see me you bring some money. Your hear?' And with that she started to walk off.

At that moment Auntie Beth came out of the chemist. 'Afternoon Miss Peek!' she called after the old woman. 'I see you've met my niece and nephew.' 'I met the boy,' Miss Peek mumbled. 'He's one of your lot all right. God help him!' She made the sign of the cross on her head and shoulders and then turned and hobbled off. Auntie Beth muttered something angrily under her breath and turned to go the other way. I waited for a moment and watched Miss Peek walking away. She looked a strange, eerie figure in her big black coat on such a sunny day.

When I caught up with Auntie Beth she didn't say anything about the strange old woman. I could sense that she was angry and didn't want to talk but I couldn't help asking. The things the old woman had said about Jimmy kept running on through my mind.

'Take no notice of Agnes Peek,' Auntie Beth said when I asked her. 'She doesn't mean any harm. The Peeks are a very old family. Agnes is the last of them. They were the richest family for miles around at one time. But that was years and years ago. Agnes still lives in the old house. The great big one up by the woods.'

Jimmy and I had seen the house on one of our walks. A huge place it was. But you'd never have thought anyone lived there. The garden was all overgrown and most of the windows had been smashed and boarded up. 'The house isn't even fit to keep animals in now,' Auntie Beth went on. 'But she won't leave it. They put her in a home a few times but she just ran away. I think they've given up with her now.' We didn't speak much after that. The shopping bags were heavy and it was quite a long walk from the village.

All the way home I thought about Agnes Peek and the things she had said about Jimmy. What did she mean when she said that she knew him? I turned around and looked for Jimmy. He was so far behind us that we had to stop to give him time to catch up. I hadn't really noticed till then just how pale and sickly he was looking.

'He's not a very strong boy, is he?' Auntie Beth said. 'He looks worse now than he did when he first arrived.' That was when it struck me. In the last few days Jimmy had grown even more like Matthew, the boy in the photograph.

'Auntie Beth,' I said quietly. 'Did Agnes Peek know Matthew when he was alive?' 'Yes she did. She knew him well.'

I kept my eye on Jimmy all evening. When it was time to go to bed I let him go up to his room first. Then, when he was asleep I went in and sat with him. He was fine at first. He was lying very still and he was breathing regularly. But as the night went on he became restless. I drew my chair right up to the bed and took hold of his hand. It was boiling. His face felt just the same – hot and dry.

I left him in the room and went into the kitchen to get a glass of water. When I got back he had kicked all the blankets off the bed and he was calling out something, but I couldn't make it out. 'Jimmy! Jimmy!' I called, shaking his arm – but he didn't wake up. Although he was kicking out he was in a very deep sleep. I poured some of the cold water into my hand and rubbed it on his face. That calmed him for a minute and I managed to drag the blankets on to the bed again.

He must have slept for about another half hour. It was a restless, fitful kind of sleep but at least he was quiet. Then he started again. This time it was worse. His breathing grew much louder and he was crying. At least I think he was crying. He was making a sort of sobbing noise but he sounded angry as well as upset. Suddenly he sat bolt upright in bed. He didn't say anything or even look at me. He just sat there like a statue. I went over to him and spoke but he didn't answer. I put my hand on his shoulder and tried to get him to lie down again. I couldn't move him. His body felt stiff.

As I was pushing him he grabbed hold of my jumper with his two fists. He pulled it so tightly that I could feel it tearing around my neck. He jerked forward and let go at the same time. I fell back from the bed and crashed into the dressing table. There was an old jug on the dressing table. It slipped off the top and smashed at my feet.

I turned on the light and looked down at the floor. The jug was in hundreds of tiny pieces. I'd never be able to fix it. 'What are you doing in here?' I looked up at the bed. Jimmy was awake and staring at me as if nothing unusual had happened.

6

It was quite clear that Jimmy had been dreaming. At least I think I'd call it dreaming. Anyway, he had no idea of what had happened so I didn't tell him. All I said was that I'd heard him calling out in his sleep and had come in to make sure he was OK. We talked for quite a long time. I left the light on and closed the curtains and we just chatted on about Mum and Dad and the new baby. Jimmy said that he wanted to go home as much as I did. He said that he'd felt ill right from the first day we arrived at Auntie Beth's. I told him that we'd soon be on our way. Everything would be fine when we got home again.

After a while he started to get sleepy so I turned out the light. I didn't want to leave him right away so I opened the curtains again to let some light into the room. There was a beautiful moon in the sky. It still wasn't quite full but it was really bright. It looked almost like the sun does sometimes on a wintry day – sort of hazy and weak.

When I was sure Jimmy was sleeping peacefully I left him and went to bed myself. I had thought of staying with him all night but I was so tired I don't think I would have been able to stay awake.

I popped my head into Jimmy's room as soon as I got up the next morning. He was still in bed fast asleep. Auntie Beth was already in the kitchen when

I went downstairs. The toast was in the grill and the room had a nice breakfasty smell. I sat down at the table and yawned.

'It's a lovely morning,' I said looking out of the window. 'I hope it stays like this for summer.'

'This is the summer!' Auntie Beth said, unlocking the back door. 'We're right in the middle of it now. Why its midsummer's day tomorrow.'

She pulled open the door and stepped out into the back. 'Just because you don't have your school holidays till August it doesn't mean that summer's not here. . . . ' Suddenly she stopped talking and made a sort of faint gasping noise. Even though I couldn't see her I could tell that something had scared her.

I jumped up and followed her out into the back. Jimmy's kitten was there – or at least what was left of it. Something had attacked it in the night. Something horrible. Its head had been torn from its body. What was left lay in bits on the ground. 'Oh God!' Auntie Beth moaned.

I managed to drag her inside and made her sit down. I put the kettle on and went upstairs to wake Jimmy. When I got to his room I saw something that made my stomach turn over. He had moved in the bed and his arm was lying on top of the blankets. There were two long deep scratches running the whole length of his forearm. The blood around the cuts had dried in dark blobs. Just like tiny blackcurrants.

I was so scared that I panicked. I grabbed some

change from my room and ran out of the house to the 'phone in the village. I wanted to go back home. Back to Mum and Dad.

There was no answer. I tried again and again but still got no reply. In the end there was nothing else I could do but go back to Auntie Beth's.

When I got back to the house Jimmy was in the back garden, right down by the stream. He had built a small fire and was burning something. It looked like his pyjamas. When he saw me he tried to hide the flames by kicking soil on to the fire. Then he waved to me. He looked thin and tired and very frightened. I did my best to smile and went up to the house. The remains of the dead kitten had gone. There was a strong smell of bleach in the air.

Auntie Beth was sitting at the kitchen table. She was trying to mend the lamp from above the back door. The frame was rusted and the glass was dirty and cracked. There were screws and bits of metal all over the table.

'I'd like to move into Jimmy's room if I can,' I said to her. 'I feel a bit lonely by myself. Would that be all right?' She looked puzzled.

'You're a bit old to be feeling lonely aren't you?' she said, staring at me. I didn't say anything. 'Still, if that's what you want. Go ahead.'

'Thanks.'

She put down the screwdriver and watched me for a moment. 'I suppose you'd better tell me,' she said at last. 'What is wrong with the lad? Is he just home-sick? Or is he really ill?' I shook my head and looked out through the window at the tiny figure in the garden. A voice was screaming inside my head. 'Why is he burning his pyjamas?' it said. 'Why?' 'I don't know what's wrong with him Auntie Beth,' I said quietly. 'I just don't know.'

7

I tried to 'phone home twice more that day. But I still didn't get through. The 'phone just rang and rang till it began to give me a headache. When the Post Office closed I went back to Auntie Beth's.

I hadn't seen much of Jimmy all day. I think he'd been keeping out of my way. He didn't say a thing all through dinner. He just sat there, playing with his food without eating. Auntie Beth didn't even notice. I could see that she was still upset about the dead kitten.

As soon as I'd finished eating I went upstairs to my room. I needed time to think things out. I was tired and confused. The holiday was turning out to be a nightmare. I hadn't been up there long when Jimmy came to the door. He was carrying his suitcase and he had his anorak tucked under his arm.

'I want to go home, Sandra,' he said, staring at me. 'I don't want to stay here any more.' I went over to him and put my arm around him. He was cold and stiff. 'Don't try and stop me!' he warned. 'I mean it!' 'If you really want to go,' I said softly, 'I won't stop you. I promise. But just tell me why first. If you still want to go after we've talked about it I won't say anything.'

We sat down on the bed and started to talk. At first, Jimmy was only crying softly but as the story came out he began to sob so loudly it was difficult to make out what he was saying. 'I can't believe it's me,' he said again and again. 'When I wake up in the morning and see the blood on my pyjamas I don't know where it's come from. It's as if someone has been playing a trick on me. I had to burn all my clothes. Every time I looked at them I felt sick.' He closed his eyes. 'I'm scared, Sandra,' he said. 'Really scared.'

I held him close to me and tried to think of something to say. He just lay there in my arms sobbing softly. When I looked down at him I couldn't believe it either. He was just a kid. A small, helpless kid.

'I'll tell you what,' I said to him. 'We'll both stay here tonight. Together. In this room. I'll stay awake all night if I have to. Then, tomorrow we can both go home.' Jimmy stared up at me. He didn't look too happy. 'It'll be all right,' I said softly. 'We couldn't go now anyway Jimmy. We'd never get a train at this time.'

We went to bed at about ten o'clock. It was a bit early but there was nothing else to do. Auntie Beth doesn't have a telly and we got sick of playing cards. Jimmy didn't bother to take his clothes off. He just kicked off his shoes and climbed into bed.

I sat by the bed and waited for him to nod off. It didn't take long. About a quarter of an hour. When I was sure he was asleep I climbed on to the bed and lay next to him. Half asleep and half awake. It was cool and peaceful just lying there with the moonlight streaming in. All the fear and horror of the day seemed to drift away.

8

It was the sound of Jimmy's breathing that woke me. A deep hoarse sound. Fast and irregular – like a dog panting. For a minute I was too scared to move. Scared, in case I might wake him. I could feel his hot breath on the back of my neck. It even had a sort of stale, animal smell.

Suddenly he grunted and threw the covers back. He jumped out of bed and scrambled over to the window. Before I could even speak he had thrown open the window and climbed up on to the ledge.

I called him – but he didn't seem to hear me. He didn't even turn around. I followed him to the window and grabbed hold of his jumper. In a flash he had turned on me, caught hold of my hair and yanked my head back. In that strange half-light I caught a glimpse of his twisted, snarling face. It was nothing like the face of the thirteen-year-old boy that I knew.

He gave a deep growl and hurled me back into the room. Then he jumped. By the time I had dragged myself up from the floor and got over to the window he was just a distant shadow running across the moonlit fields.

I went into my room, put on my boots and coat and grabbed my torch from the wardrobe drawer. The dagger with the crucifix handle was still lying on the floor in the corner. I saw it just before I left the room. I picked it up, shoved it into my pocket and crept downstairs to the front door.

From far away there came a sound that made my blood run chill. A long, low howl that seemed to fill the stillness of the night. I heard it twice and then it stopped. It was followed by the sound of farm dogs all barking madly.

I left the house and turned in the direction I had seen Jimmy go.

9

I walked very slowly. My hand was on the dagger in my pocket, ready in case anything jumped out at me from the shadows. It was a warm, close night. The huge moon hung low and heavy in the black sky. I felt it watching me like a great evil eye. I felt lonely and scared. Even the sound of my own footsteps frightened me, but I kept listening and looking for a sign of Jimmy.

After about an hour I began to give up. I was tired and so far had seen or heard nothing. Then I came across the bird. It was a swan or maybe a goose. It was so torn and battered, I couldn't properly tell. Its neck had been snapped like a twig and one of its wings was stretched right out, like an arm reaching to grab something. There were feathers, streaked with red all over the grass. I knew then that Jimmy had passed that way before me.

I hadn't gone much further when I saw a pale, flickering light shining from a house in the distance. As I got nearer I recognized the crumbling chimneys and the broken windows. It was Agnes Peek's house. Perhaps I'd been heading there all the time without realizing it. Anyway, the minute I saw it I knew that only she would be able to help me now.

I looked in my pocket to see if I had any money. There was a £1 note there. I held it tightly in my fist and set off for the house. The light I had seen was at the back in a small window by a low wooden door. It must have been the servants' entrance at one time. I banged on the door and pushed it open.

She was sitting by an empty fireplace. There was an old lamp standing on a table by the wall. Its warm yellow light made the room look warm and inviting. 'I knew you'd come tonight,' she said turning to face me. 'I've already heard him up on the hills.' She held out her grubby hand to me. 'Have you brought me some money?'

I stepped into the room and stuffed the £1 note into her hand. There was a stale, musty smell in the room. The bits of furniture I could see were dirty and worn-looking. There was no carpet. An empty bottle lay on the floor by her feet.

'I was about your age the last time,' she said. 'That was over fifty years ago. The moon was full and it was midsummer night. Just like tonight. I found Matthew in the woods. Well, first I heard him howling then I found him with his leg caught in a trap. Lucky for me that he'd walked into a fox trap. He would have killed me if he'd been free. The men from the village dragged him up here. Frothing at the mouth, he was. Just like a mad dog. They had to tie him down with ropes and send for his mother.'

She stopped talking for a moment and looked up at me as if she'd forgotten who I was. Her gaze was unsteady and her watery eyes shone in the lamplight. She looked drunk. 'Only his mother didn't come,' she went on at last. 'The father did. But he was too late. Poor Matthew was already dead when he got here. The madness had killed him.

'One of the men had a knife. A cruel looking thing it was – with a cross and the figure of Jesus on its handle. They said that it would free Matthew's soul from the evil that had taken it. Without it he would find no rest. His soul would rise up from the grave and wander the hills in the form of a wolf. So, they drove the knife into his dead body and left it there.'

I took the dagger out of my pocket and put it down before her. For a long time she didn't say anything. She just turned it over and over in her hands, murmuring softly to herself. At last she put it down. 'I knew that she'd kept it,' she said. 'She told me herself. It broke her heart when the boy died. She was never the same after that. There's always been bad blood in the Carter family. It comes from way back. People forget it's there till it comes back again.'

'Is that what's happened to Jimmy?' I asked her. 'Is he the same as Matthew?' 'Just the same,' she said nodding. 'I saw it in his face that first minute. It always shows itself in the boys and always when they are thirteen years old. When the boy is becoming a man – that's when it strikes him down. After tonight it will be all over. When the moon dies it'll take the boy with him. The madness in his blood will burn him out. Just like a fire cracker. He will die.'

'But isn't there anything we can do to stop it?' I said grabbing her hand. 'We must be able to help him. Jimmy doesn't even know what he's doing!' She got up from her chair and shuffled over to the window. 'You see that,' she said pointing up to the moon. 'That is what causes it. The midsummer night's moon. If you want to save him you must blind him to the moonlight.'

I didn't need to hear any more. 'Just tell me where I'll find him,' I asked her. 'That's all I want to know.' 'He'll be on the very top of the hills,' she said. 'That's where the pull is strongest. On high ground.'

She moved back from the window and picked up the dagger. 'Take this with you,' she said, handing it to me. 'If the boy dies you must use it. For his sake!' Her voice was suddenly very hard. 'Even if you save this boy tonight you may still need the dagger,' she warned me. 'One day the madness may return. One day when you least expect it. Maybe it's better to let him die now. Now that you have the dagger and are ready.'

I didn't even bother to answer. Minutes later I was out running across the damp fields towards the hills.

10

I was tired. Tired and cold. Inside the house the things that Agnes Peek had said seemed to make sense. Out in the cold night air they sounded silly. An old woman's ramblings. I turned my collar up against the cool breeze and walked on towards the top of the hills.

From far away I heard the sound of a police siren. At first it was only very faint but it got louder and louder as it came up the road towards the hills. Soon, I could see it racing on behind me, its blue light flashing wildly. I got down behind a bush and waited for it to pass.

From then on the stillness of the night was broken. I could hear the sounds of doors banging as people came out to discover what was going on. As I climbed higher I could see the lights in the farmhouses spread out across the valley. People were awake.

There were other sounds too. An owl calling out in the night. Cows mooing in the fields and the dogs yelping and barking in every farmhouse yard for miles around. And last of all the same wolf-like howl that I'd heard earlier. Only this time it was much nearer. Jimmy wasn't far away.

When I got to the very top of the hill I saw him. He was completely alone. A black shape against the huge silver moon. He was standing on one leg, perched like a stork and staring up at the moon, howling softly.

He looked so strange and sad that at first all I could do was stand there and watch him with a lump in my throat. Then I saw something move out of the corner of my eye. It was a police dog. It came tearing across the open fields, silent as a shadow.

I called out to Jimmy and started to run over to him. Suddenly, he let out a low growl and turned to face me. I froze with fear. His cruel eyes flashed red like fire in the darkness. They stared at me with a kind of hunger. A hunger for blood. His lips parted and he opened his mouth wide baring his sharp teeth. There was blood, fresh from a kill smeared around his mouth. 'Jimmy. It's me. Sandra,' I said softly. He didn't even hear me. The creature in front of me wasn't Jimmy. It was a wild animal. A mad, wild animal. And it would kill me if it could.

The growling got louder. It started to froth at the mouth as it rocked to and fro watching me as a cat watches a mouse. It jerked forward. I covered my face with my hands and screamed.

When I looked again the police dog was there. For a moment it stood between me and Jimmy with its head down. Then it jumped at him. He went crashing to the ground with the dog on top of him. Together they rolled on the grass growling and tearing at each other.

By the time I got to them they were both soaked in a mixture of blood and froth. And Jimmy was hurt. Badly hurt. I began to cry. Glad and sorry at the same time. He was hurt but now it was safe to go near him. He couldn't harm me now.

I picked up a stick I had found in the field and beat the dog till it let go of him and ran out of my reach. Jimmy was still making all sorts of strange noises. It was hard to tell the difference between his growls and the dog's. Still swinging the stick through the air to keep the dog away I managed to get my coat off. I threw it over Jimmy's head so that he couldn't see the moon. The growling stopped and he lay on the ground without moving.

From further down the hill I could hear the sounds of men's voices. The dog ran off towards them barking. I went over to Jimmy, pulled him to his feet and dragged him away – making sure the coat stayed over his head.

I think he must have been in some sort of a trance because he didn't make a sound. His arm was broken and he was bleeding all over – but he didn't seem to feel it. I didn't try to make him talk. I just headed for home as quickly as I could get him to move.

The men were following us now. I don't think they had seen us, but I could hear them quite clearly. Once or twice I saw the beam of their flashlight as it came over the top of the hill.

It was no good. They were gaining on us. Getting closer and closer. I pulled Jimmy into a ditch at the bottom of the hill and hid there, waiting for them to pass.

There were two of them. Two policemen with a radio and a torch each. They were walking down the hillside about a hundred metres apart. The dog was running between the two of them sniffing at the ground. 'I'm going to try the fields on the other side of the hill,' one of them called out. 'I saw some sheep down there. It might have gone after them!' 'OK!' the other policeman called back.

The dog was getting nearer to us. I couldn't see it but I could hear it whining softly. As it got nearer the whining grew louder and it began to sound excited. Soon it was only a few metres from the ditch.

I took the dagger out of my pocket and held it in front of me like a soldier ready to charge into battle. Then I waited.

When the dog found us it started barking its head off. I dragged Jimmy up from the floor and tried to climb out of the ditch. But I didn't get far. The dog jumped at me and sank its teeth deep into my arm. Pain shot through me like an electric shock. For a minute I couldn't keep my balance. The ground started to spin around me. I thought I was going to be sick but instead I fell on top of Jimmy and fainted.

11

I was in bed when I woke up. Back at Auntie Beth's. The sun was shining in through the lace curtains. When I tried to sit up I felt a stab of pain in my shoulder. There was a large white bandage where the police dog had bitten me. Everything that had happened the night before suddenly came back to me.

There was nobody else in the house. Jimmy's room was empty and Auntie Beth wasn't in the kitchen. There was just a note on the sideboard. It said:

Gone to the hospital with Jimmy. Stay in bed till I get back. If you're hungry you can make yourself something to eat but I'll be back at lunch time.

Auntie Beth.

PS Your father will be here later on today. You've got a new baby brother.

I didn't feel like anything to eat so I went back to sleep and waited to see what would happen. I was so worn out I didn't even have the energy to worry about Jimmy.

The next few days were a mess. Jimmy was in hospital. He was in a coma and he didn't wake up for two whole days. The police came to Auntie Beth's on both of those days and asked me about

Jimmy. I tried to tell them the truth. I told them that he'd been feeling ill ever since we'd arrived at Auntie Beth's and I told them that Jimmy walked in his sleep. The only thing I didn't tell them was that I thought he was a werewolf. There was no point telling them that. They wouldn't have believed me. They'd just have thought I was crazy. So I didn't say anything about that part of it. I left it up to the police to work out what had happened.

When Jimmy did come out of the hospital he looked a lot better. He was fatter and the tiredness had gone from around his eyes. He didn't ever talk about that night the police had found us on the hills. Nobody did. Auntie Beth didn't say a word about it and neither did Dad. They acted as if it had never happened.

It's been like that ever since. That summer is just a memory now. A shadow from the past. Each year it gets paler and paler. Maybe that's for the best. I don't know.

I've still got the dagger. I keep it by my bed. When midsummer night comes around I don't go to sleep. I just sit there in the darkness. Waiting. I think of Jimmy and I think of the baby. My little baby brother. What will happen when he is thirteen? One day I know that I'm going to hear that long, blood-hungry howl ringing out across the fields from the top of a hill somewhere.

Only this time I'll be ready . . . .